MW01196064

COOL CASTLES AND PALACES
KING LUDWIG'S CASTLE

by Clara Bennington

pogo

Ideas for Parents and Teachers

Pogo Books let children practice reading informational text while introducing them to nonfiction features such as headings, labels, sidebars, maps, and diagrams, as well as a table of contents, glossary, and index.

Carefully leveled text with a strong photo match offers early fluent readers the support they need to succeed.

Before Reading

- "Walk" through the book and point out the various nonfiction features. Ask the student what purpose each feature serves.
- Look at the glossary together. Read and discuss the words.

Read the Book

- Have the child read the book independently.
- Invite him or her to list questions that arise from reading.

After Reading

- Discuss the child's questions. Talk about how he or she might find answers to those questions.
- Prompt the child to think more. Ask: King Ludwig's castle is also known as Neuschwanstein Castle. What more would you like to learn about this castle?

Pogo Books are published by Jump!
5357 Penn Avenue South
Minneapolis, MN 55419
www.jumplibrary.com

Library of Congress Cataloging-in-Publication Data

Names: Bennington, Clara, author.
Title: King Ludwig's castle / by Clara Bennington.
Description: Minneapolis, MN: Pogo Books are published by Jump!, [2020] | Series: Cool Castles and Palaces
Audience: Ages: 7-10. | Includes index.
Identifiers: LCCN 2018056980 (print)
LCCN 2019002855 (ebook)
ISBN 9781641288705 (ebook)
ISBN 9781641288699 (hardcover : alk. paper)
Subjects: LCSH: Castles—Juvenile literature.
Ludwig II, King of Bavaria, 1845-1886—Juvenile literature.
Classification: LCC GT3550 (ebook)
LCC GT3550 .B46 2020 (print) | DDC 728.8109433—dc23
LC record available at https://lccn.loc.gov/2018056980

Editor: Jenna Trnka
Designer: Molly Ballanger

Photo Credits: Alessandro Colle/Shutterstock, cover; Alberto Masnovo/Shutterstock, 1; Pres Panayotov/Shutterstock, 3; Universal Images/SuperStock, 4; Mikhail Markovskiy/Shutterstock, 5; canadastock/Shutterstock, 6-7; Elena Korchenko/All Canada Photos/SuperStock, 8-9; Michael F. Schönitzer, 10; mironov/Shutterstock, 11; Igor Plotnikov/Shutterstock, 12-13; ClickAlps Srls/Alamy, 14-15; dpa picture alliance/Alamy, 16, 18-19; Norman Barrett/Alamy, 17; cge2010/Shutterstock, 20-21; Francesco Carucci/Shutterstock, 23.

Printed in the United States of America at Corporate Graphics in North Mankato, Minnesota.

TABLE OF CONTENTS

CHAPTER 1

A FAIRYTALE CASTLE

Ludwig II became king of Bavaria, a state of Germany, when he was 19 years old. Some called him Mad King Ludwig. Why? He liked to be alone. He had ideas that people thought were unusual.

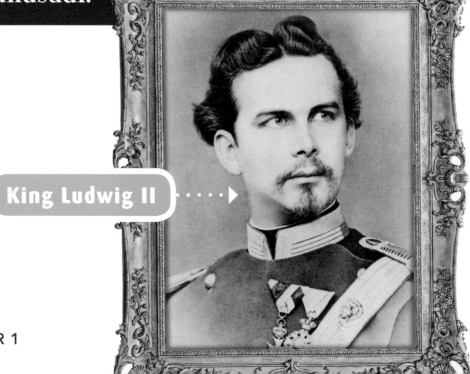

King Ludwig II ·····▶

Like what? Having **grottos** built into his castles. These rooms look like caves. They have colorful lighting. One has a waterfall. Another has a pond.

Ludwig wanted a new castle high atop a rocky cliff. It would be in the Bavarian Alps. He wanted it to look like it was from the **Middle Ages**. Construction began in 1869.

DID YOU KNOW?

Walt Disney visited King Ludwig's castle. Some say it inspired his ideas for Sleeping Beauty Castle at Disneyland. Cinderella Castle in Disney World also looks a lot like it!

Throne Room

The castle looked old. But it had the most advanced technology of the time. Steel supports hold up the **vaulted** ceilings in the **Throne** Room. An electric bell system called for servants. An elevator carried food from the kitchen up to the dining room.

WHAT DO YOU THINK?

The castle also had hot water. The toilets flushed. The castle was connected to phone lines. But not many people even had phones at this time! What new technology would you add to your home?

CHAPTER 2
MANY MURALS

King Ludwig hired the best artists to paint **murals** on the walls of his castle. This one is in the Throne Room.

mural ····▶

study

Murals are in his study, too. A desk is here. His writing set is still on it! He kept his plans for the castle in a cupboard here.

The Singers' Hall is covered in murals. This hall was never actually used for singing. King Ludwig wanted the large room to honor the **legends** he loved.

WHAT DO YOU THINK?

King Ludwig wanted to be surrounded by pictures of things that were important to him. Do you keep pictures of things you like on your walls? What are they of?

Step into the king's dressing room. The murals here show the lives of two poets the king liked. Look at the room off to the side. It is called an **oriel**. The king's jewelry box is here!

poets

oriel

CHAPTER 3

· ·

THE SWAN KING

Swans are **symbols** of **purity**. They held a special meaning for King Ludwig. They are in his family's **coat of arms**. Images of swans are found all around the castle. The castle's name is Neuschwanstein. It means "new swan castle."

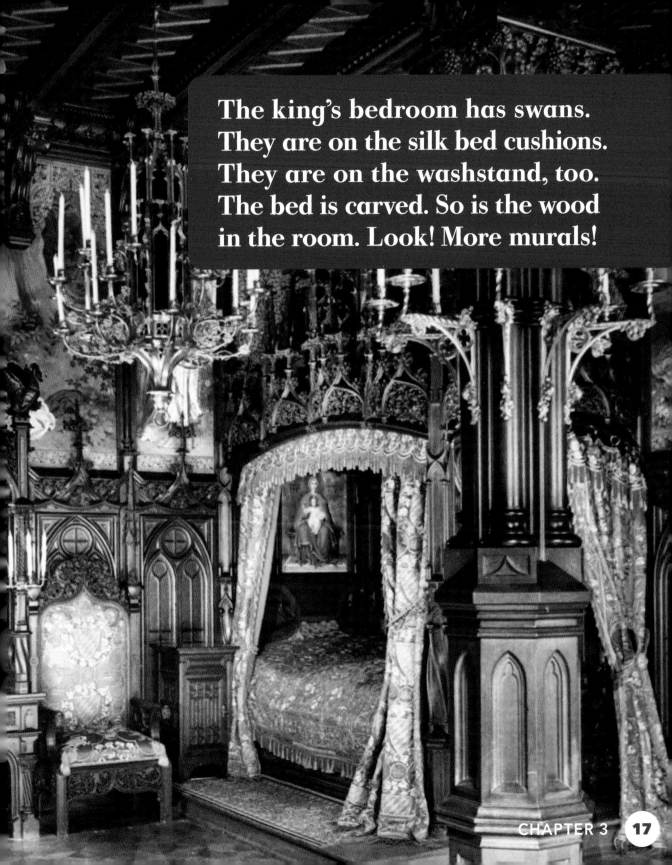

The king's bedroom has swans. They are on the silk bed cushions. They are on the washstand, too. The bed is carved. So is the wood in the room. Look! More murals!

King Louis IX

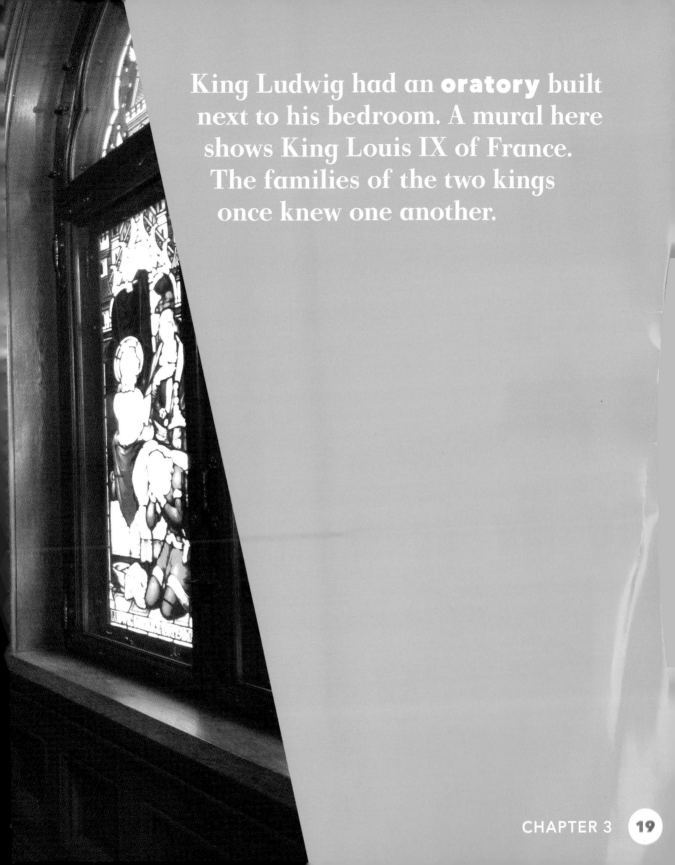

King Ludwig had an **oratory** built next to his bedroom. A mural here shows King Louis IX of France. The families of the two kings once knew one another.

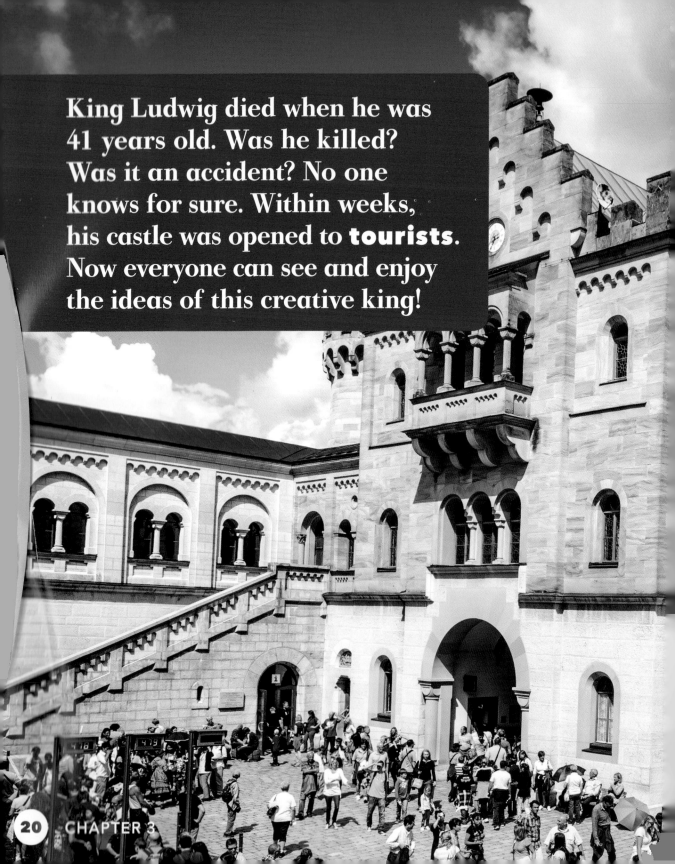

King Ludwig died when he was 41 years old. Was he killed? Was it an accident? No one knows for sure. Within weeks, his castle was opened to **tourists**. Now everyone can see and enjoy the ideas of this creative king!

TAKE A LOOK!

King Ludwig died before the castle was finished. Only 14 of the 200 rooms were completed. What rooms can visitors see?

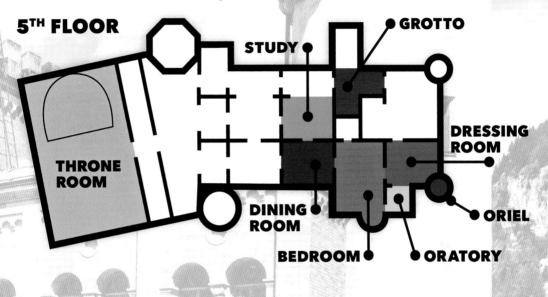

5TH FLOOR

- STUDY
- GROTTO
- THRONE ROOM
- DRESSING ROOM
- DINING ROOM
- ORIEL
- BEDROOM
- ORATORY

6TH FLOOR

SINGERS' HALL

QUICK FACTS & TOOLS

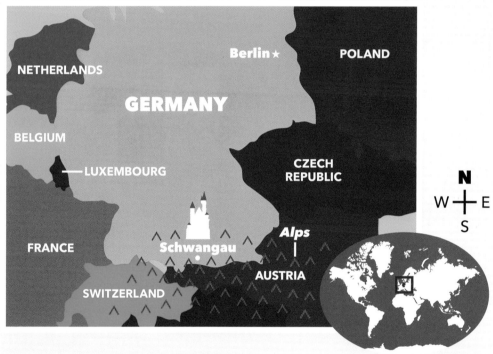

KING LUDWIG'S CASTLE (NEUSCHWANSTEIN)

Location:
Schwangau, Germany

Year Construction Began: 1869

Size: 1.5 acres (0.6 hectares)

Number of Finished Rooms: 14

Primary Architects:
Eduard Riedel, Georg von Dollmann, Julius Hofmann

Average Number of Visitors Each Year: 1.4 million

coat of arms: A design on a shield that identifies a noble family or person, a city, or an organization.

grottos: Small indoor structures built to look like caves.

legends: Stories handed down from earlier times, sometimes based on fact but not entirely true.

Middle Ages: The period of European history from approximately 1000 to 1450 CE.

murals: Large paintings done on walls.

oratory: A private chapel or place of prayer.

oriel: A large bay window that projects from a wall.

purity: The state or quality of being clean or innocent or free from evil or guilt.

symbols: Objects or designs that stand for, suggest, or represent something else.

throne: A special chair for a ruler to sit on during a ceremony.

tourists: People who travel and visit places for pleasure.

vaulted: In the form of an arch.

INDEX

TO LEARN MORE

Finding more information is as easy as 1, 2, 3.

1 Go to www.factsurfer.com

2 Enter "KingLudwig'sCastle" into the search box.

3 Choose your book to see a list of websites.

FACT SURFER